BLOSSOMS IN WINTER

14 DESIGNS IN WOOL-FELT APPLIQUÉ

PATTI EATON AND PAMELA MOSTEK

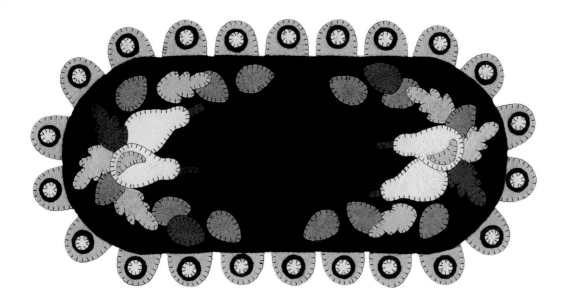

Martingale™
& COMPANY

Credits

President . . . . Nancy J. Martin
CEO . . . . Daniel J. Martin
Publisher . . . . Jane Hamada
Editorial Director . . . . Mary V. Green
Managing Editor . . . . .Tina Cook
Technical Editor . . . . Ursula Reikes
Copy Editor . . . . Liz McGehee
Design Director . . . . Stan Green
Illustrator . . . . Robin Strobel
Assistant Illustrator . . . . Lisa McKenney
Text Designer . . . . Jennifer LaRock Shontz
Cover Designer . . . . Stan Green
Photographer . . . . Brent Kane

That Patchwork Place® is an imprint of
Martingale & Company™.

Blossoms in Winter: 14 Designs in Wool-Felt Appliqué
© 2002 by Patti Eaton and Pamela Mostek

Martingale & Company
20205 144th Avenue NE
Woodinville, WA 98072-8478 USA
www.martingale-pub.com

Printed in Hong Kong
07 06 05 04 03 02   8 7 6 5 4 3 2

**Library of Congress Cataloging-in-Publication data is available
upon request.**

ISBN 1-56477-423-6

Dedication

To each and every quilter and crafter who pursues the art of
needlework in this age of high technology. It is this love of
creating beautiful things that will leave a rich heritage for
those who follow.

Acknowledgments

Our sincere thanks go out to everyone who encouraged us to
share our experience and ideas in this book. We appreciate
your confidence! A special thanks from both of us goes to:

Michalina Centofanti at National Nonwovens, for sup-
plying us not only with their wonderful products to work
with, but also with enthusiasm, information, and support for
our designs.

Everyone at Martingale & Company who supported our
idea of a book using wool-felt appliqué and allowed us to put
it together in record time!

Patti would also like to thank:

The "Gallery Girls" at my quilt shop, Hawthorne
Gallery, for the extra hours they put in so that I would have
time to devote to the book.

My good friend and coauthor, Pam Mostek. Without her
push, I would never have had the courage and confidence to
tackle a book.

My son, Dusty, who is always willing to lend his technical
assistance, whether it is a digital camera or a new computer
program. It has saved me hours of frustration and aggravation.

My husband, Lester, who is never fazed by my ventures
and who thinks that I can do it all. Your support and efforts
have not gone unnoticed.

Pam would also like to thank:

My good friend and coauthor, Patti Eaton, for years of
great projects together. It's nice to have someone who always
speaks my language!

My daughter Rachel, for always cheerfully helping me
out with design feedback, cutting, stitching, errand running,
record keeping, and any other little task I need help with. But
most especially, thanks for your faith in your mom!

My daughter Stacey, who always offers her quick eye for
design when needed. I appreciate your long-distance encour-
agement and confidence in whatever Mom is creating!

My husband, Bob, for giving up many fun, summer-cabin
weekends so I could stay immersed in the world of wool felt.

Mission Statement

We are dedicated to providing quality products
and service by working together to inspire
creativity and to enrich the lives we touch.

CONTENTS

A LITTLE BACKGROUND

So, you may be asking yourself, just how did a couple of quilters like Pam and Patti end up in the wonderful world of wool felt? Very easily, is our answer. As quilters and quilt designers, we are always in search of something new, eye-catching, richly colored, and of course, not too time-consuming. Like everyone else, we want to create and design the kind of projects that are so beautiful they must certainly have taken a lot of time, when actually they didn't. Sound familiar?

When we began to experiment with wool felt, we were looking for just this kind of thing, and we loved what we discovered. We found the same wonderful rich quality as wool, yet with some added advantages. First, we love the fantastic range of colors that are available in wool felt. Everything from deep, rich heathered fall tones to softly shaded pastels. The variety of beautiful colors that are available from our supplier, National Nonwovens, has been very exciting and fun to work with. We love the added body of wool felt, too. Projects hold their shape well and don't need to be stabilized or interfaced to add extra body.

And then, of course, there is the big important factor of cost. Wool felt is less expensive than 100 percent–woven wool cloth—definitely a good thing for quilters! We're always looking for the most practical way to make beautiful projects.

So with all these things in mind, we began creating. And we loved the results! Not only were we pleased with the wonderful projects we made for our homes, but many of these projects also took far less time than making a quilt. And the wool-felt appliqué technique simply couldn't be easier. Just cut out the shapes and blanket stitch them. Because wool felt doesn't fray, there's no need to turn under the edges.

Of course, once we discovered how simple and fun working with wool felt was, we were anxious to share our ideas. We were convinced that quilters and crafters alike would love the ease and simplicity of working with this fabric. We each designed and published patterns using wool felt for our individual design companies, but we knew putting a group of lovely, easy-to-make-and-use designs together in a book would be a great way to show quilters the wide range of possibilities.

Over the years, we have tackled dozens of fun projects together, so we thought, why not a book? With the help of the folks at Martingale & Company, we are bringing these projects to you in *Blossoms in Winter*. We hope you are going to be as excited to try some of them as we have been to experiment and design with this new fabric.

So take a few minutes to browse through the pages and discover just what exciting projects are in store for you when you enter the wonderful world of wool felt. We're pretty confident you're going to enjoy this new adventure!

—Patti and Pam

WELCOME TO THE WORLD OF WOOL FELT

Wool felt is simple and fun to use. The techniques are straightforward, the colors are gorgeous, and the results are outstanding. You'll be able to easily create projects whose rich touches of color will add unique, handmade-looking accents to your home in a minimum of time. What could be better?

Winter is the perfect season for these lovely wool-felt projects. The warm feel of wool felt and the deep heathered colors make it a natural for this time of year. And for a different wintertime twist, we've designed many of the projects with appliqués of flowers, leaves, and vines. Who said blossoms were only for springtime?

We've included a variety of different projects, so you should be able to find some that are perfect for you. There are table runners and wall hangings, decorator pillows, and even two lovely lap-sized throws to snuggle under in the cold weather. And what winter book would

be complete without a collection of Christmas projects? Our "Poinsettia Wall Hanging and Mantel Cover" and "Winter Rose Tree Skirt" will add an elegant holiday accent to your home.

Because we're quilters at heart, like many of you, one of the goals for our book was to use some of our favorite quilting tricks and techniques with wool felt. You'll find blanket-stitch appliqué and reverse appliqué too. We've done a little machine quilting on some of the projects and added cotton bindings to others. We're very pleased with the projects where we combined wool felt with gorgeous printed flannels and cottons too. And for you handwork lovers, we've done some embellishing with pearl cotton to add a special touch.

The blanket-stitch appliqué we have used in the book can be done by hand or by machine, whichever is your preference. We both love the blanket stitch done by our Pfaff sewing machines, so we usually choose machine blanket stitching. However, we always keep a small hand-stitching project handy in the car or by the couch, just so we don't waste any valuable stitching time. There's still something very relaxing about the hand-stitching process.

Wool-felt projects are also a great place to add a little hand embellishing if that's one of your favorite pastimes. We've used pearl cotton to add accents to several of the designs in the book, but any of them would look wonderful with a little handwork added. Let your imagination go wild. Embroidery stitches of all kinds, wool yarn, buttons, cording—they look wonderful added to a wool-felt design.

Take a few minutes to read "Wool-Felt Basics" on page 6 before you begin your project. You'll see that the techniques for working with wool felt couldn't be easier; just prepare the fabric, cut out, glue, and stitch! In a very short time, you'll have a wall hanging or a decorator pillow that will add a unique, handmade accent to any spot in your home. Happy stitching!

It's easy to create lovely projects using wool felt. The techniques are simple, and most projects can be completed in a short time. Here we've included some basic tips and instructions to assist you as you follow the instructions for each project.

TOOLS AND SUPPLIES

In addition to the standard sewing supplies, such as regular sewing thread, scissors, rotary-cutting equipment, and pins, we have put together a list of additional notions you'll need to complete the wool-felt projects in this book. Some are not necessary for every project, so read through the directions for your project before you begin.

❖ Template plastic for making templates of often used appliqué shapes
❖ Freezer paper for making paper patterns
❖ Quilter's marking pencils in white, yellow, or silver for marking the felt
❖ String to use with a marking pencil for drawing circles on the felt
❖ Fabric glue to hold smaller appliqué shapes in place before stitching
❖ Basting spray for securing large appliqué shapes in place or large pieces of felt together before stitching. Read the manufacturer's directions and use in a well-ventilated space.
❖ Pinking shears or rotary wave blade to create a decorative edge (if required for the project you're making)
❖ Heavy thread (30 weight), such as YLI Jeanstitch, for topstitching or blanket stitching by machine
❖ Pearl cotton for hand-embroidered stitches

SELECTING THE FABRIC

When you're shopping for wool felt, you may find bolts with different percentages of wool and rayon. Our favorite wool-rayon blends, from National Nonwovens, are the ones with 20 or 35 percent wool. After wetting and drying, both of these are transformed into a soft, easy-to-work-with fabric.

The blends with 50 or 70 percent wool are also lovely, but they are thicker after soaking and drying, which makes them slightly more difficult to appliqué. We recommend that you select fabrics with either 20 or 35 percent wool, which are also the two blends most commonly found in quilt shops in a variety of rich colors.

PREPARING THE FABRIC

If this is your first adventure in wool felt, you might be a little skeptical about the fabric as you find it lined up on the shelves of your local quilt shop. Don't worry; the wool felt that you purchase will look and feel nothing like the soft, luxurious fabric that you'll create after you've prepared it for sewing.

The first step is to soak your fabric for a few minutes in warm water. We recommend soaking each color separately because dye will be discharged as the wool felt soaks, especially with the darker colors. A quick and easy way to soak your fabric is to use the basin of your washing machine. Add enough warm water to cover the fabric and allow it to sit for a few minutes to absorb the water, moving it around gently with your hands as it soaks. Do not let the washer begin to agitate. Just soaking is all that's needed. (Of course, for smaller pieces, you can also soak your wool felt in the sink or even a bucket or large pan if you prefer.)

Carefully squeeze out the excess water over the washing machine. Remove as much water as you can without stretching and pulling on the fabric. After you've removed the fabric, you may want to run a little hot water into the machine and then drain it out to be sure you are rid of all the dye.

The next step is to toss the fabric into the dryer to fluff and soften the fibers. Dry your wool felt until it is *almost* dry. Taking it out when it is almost dry is a good way to avoid overdrying if your dryer temperature is too

hot. Depending on the size of the piece, it could take 20 to 30 minutes. You may want to experiment with a few scraps to see the results from your own dryer. If the fabric appears slightly fuzzy, turn down the heat slightly or don't dry it quite so long.

If you only need to dry one or two small pieces, throw an old towel into the dryer with the pieces to prevent the wool felt from wrinkling into a ball. Be sure to use an old towel because some dye may be discharged while the wool felt is wet.

When you remove the almost-dry wool felt from the dryer, lay the fabric out flat until it is completely dry. If you want a textured, country look, smooth out the wrinkles with your hand as the fabric dries. For a smoother look, iron it lightly after it is dry. It's fun to experiment with achieving different textures through drying, so you might want to try a few small test pieces until you achieve just the look you're after.

You'll notice when your wool felt is dry that it has shrunk from the original size. The amount of shrinkage will vary, depending on the length of drying time and/or the heat of your dryer.

DETERMINING YARDAGE REQUIREMENTS

Wool felt is available in two widths: 36" and 72". Be sure to notice which width is required for your project to make sure you purchase the right amount of fabric. Many stores also carry wool felt in 9" x 12" or 12" x 18" pieces. These are great for the small pieces used in the projects.

Extra yardage has been added to all fabric requirements to allow for the shrinkage that occurs when you prepare the wool felt for sewing.

DRAWING A CIRCLE

Several of the projects in this book include appliqué shapes arranged in a circular design. With a piece of string and a marking pencil, you can easily and quickly draw a circle of any size.

1. Start with a square of wool felt (or a piece of freezer paper) cut to the size indicated for the project you are making. Fold the square in half vertically, then in half horizontally, and mark the center.
2. Tie a piece of string around the marking pencil. Make a knot the required distance from the marking pencil. This distance is the radius of the circle and is given for each circle you need to make. The radius is one-half of the diameter, so an 18" radius results in a 36"-diameter circle; a 2½" radius results in a 5"-diameter circle.
3. Hold the knot at the center mark on the square and carefully draw a circle with the marking pencil.

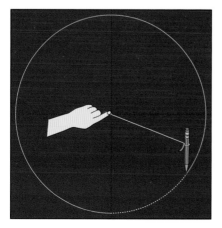

ADDING THE APPLIQUÉS

Preparing appliqué shapes for stitching is simple. Because the fabric is the same on both sides, you don't need to worry about reversing the appliqués. Either side will work equally well. Another wonderful quality of wool felt is the amount of give to the fabric. This flexibility is what allows you to use straight strips of fabric for the vines and circles; you can simply ease the strips gently around the circles. It also allows you to manipulate the appliqué shapes by turning the leaf on a stem, for example, until you are pleased with the arrangement.

If you want to adapt the designs to use with hand appliqué, remember that you won't be able to turn and adjust cotton pieces the same way you can manipulate wool felt. You'll also need to add a ¼" turn-under allowance on each shape.

The cut edges of wool felt don't fray, so turning under appliqués or using fusible webbing is not necessary. Just cut out the shapes, and then follow these simple steps:

1. Make plastic templates of the patterns, especially if you'll be repeating an appliqué shape more than a few times. Straight strips of felt for vines and circles don't require patterns, since they are simply straight pieces of felt. Because the felt is flexible, the strips can be gently eased around a circle without having to be cut on the bias grain.
2. Trace around the appliqué shapes onto the uncoated (non-shiny) side of freezer paper.
3. Iron the freezer paper with the drawn shape onto the wool felt. Using sharp scissors, cut out the shape through the paper and wool felt. Using the freezer paper not only makes tracing much easier, but it helps you cut out a sharp, clean shape.

Freezer paper

4. Remove the paper and position the shapes on the background. Place strips for vines and circles first, gently easing the straight strips around the circle and overlapping the ends as needed. Refer to the color photos and placement guides for the project you are making to arrange the appliqué shapes.

5. Secure the pieces lightly with fabric glue. Just a drop or two will hold them until you stitch them to the background. If your appliqué shape has more than one layer, position, glue, and stitch the first layer; then position, glue, and stitch the next layer. Keep adding layers until the appliqué is complete.

> **TIP** Feel free to alter the number of appliqué shapes within the projects to suit your taste. Play with the shapes until you are pleased with the arrangement.

Stitching

Many of the appliqué shapes are secured to the background with a blanket stitch. This has its roots in the American folk art of penny rugs, which were often blanket stitched by hand.

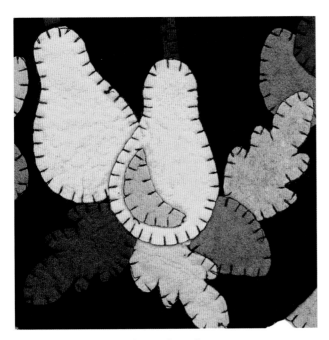

Blanket-stitch appliqué

For a slightly different look, we appliquéd some of the projects with straight stitching.

Straight-stitch appliqué

We machine appliquéd all of the projects in the book, but any of them could easily be hand appliquéd if you prefer. Machine blanket stitching will give a more uniform look and is, of course, much faster. Blanket stitching your project by hand will allow you to create a unique, folk-art look by varying the length and width of your stitches. See "Using Embroidery Stitches" on page 51.

You can use either method to stitch the appliqué shapes to the background, depending on the effect you want. You may even want to experiment with other types of decorative embroidery stitching on your appliqué shapes. The choice is yours!

CARING FOR YOUR CREATION

To keep your wool-felt creation looking beautiful for many years, there are just a few tips to keep in mind. First, don't iron the front of your project once it is completed. Ironing will flatten the texture and might make the felt shiny in places. Try gently steaming from the wrong side, if necessary, to remove fold lines or wrinkles. If pressing seems necessary, place a heavy towel on the ironing board, place your project right side down on the towel, and press lightly on the back.

We recommend dry cleaning if it's necessary to clean your creation once it has been stitched together.

WINTER ROSE TREE SKIRT

WINTER ROSE TREE SKIRT by Pamela Mostek. Our first inspiration for the book was a holiday tree skirt. We just knew wool felt would be perfect for creating a tree skirt with an elegant, unusual look, and we were right. For a little touch of the nontraditional for Christmas, we created it with winter roses.

Materials

Yardages are based on 72"-wide wool felt and 42"-wide cotton.

1⅓ yds. dark red felt for background

¼ yd. white felt for roses

½ yd. dark green felt for stems and leaves

1⅓ yds. felt for backing

3 pieces, each 12" x 18", light green felt for vine circle

Scrap of gold felt for flower centers

Scrap of red felt for berries

⅔ yd. cotton for binding

Heavy thread (for machine topstitching) or pearl cotton (for hand stitching)

Template plastic

Freezer paper

34" length of string

Quilter's marking pencil

Fabric glue

Assembling the Tree Skirt

Referring to "Preparing the Fabric" on page 6, prepare the wool felt for cutting and sewing. Use the appliqué patterns on page 57.

1. Cut a 38" x 38" square of dark red felt for the background. Fold the square in half horizontally, then in half vertically, and mark the center. Referring to "Drawing a Circle" on page 8, Make a knot in the string 18" from the marking pencil and draw a 36"-diameter circle on the square. Cut out the circle on the drawn line.

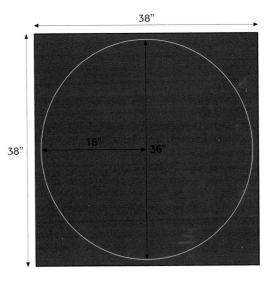

2. Make a knot in the string 13" from the marking pencil and draw a second circle, 26" in diameter, to use as an appliqué placement guide.

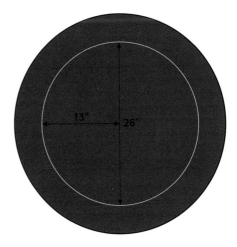

3. Make a knot in the string 2½" from the marking pencil and draw a third circle, 5" in diameter, to cut out for the tree trunk. With a long ruler and rotary cutter, cut a line from the outside edge to the center circle. With scissors, cut out the center circle.

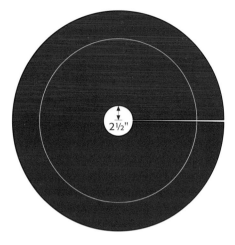

4. Cut enough light green strips, ½" wide, to go around the vine circle (approximately 90"). Place the strips around the circle, overlapping the ends as needed to complete the circle. Straight stitch around the inside edge of the strips.

5. Referring to "Adding the Appliqués" on page 8, cut and position the appliqué shapes around the vine circle. Adjust the leaf-and-stem shapes slightly as needed to fit the circle. Tuck the ends of each stem

under the outside edge of the circle. Straight stitch around all the appliqué shapes, including the outside edge of the circle to secure the ends of the stems.

12 dark green leaves and stems (Template 1)

12 white roses (Template 2)

12 gold flower centers (Template 3)

30 red berries (Template 4)

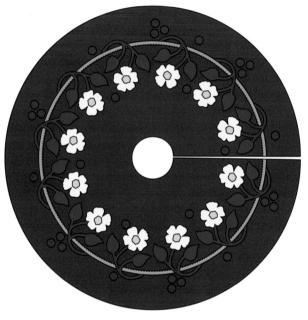

Placement Guide

Finishing the Tree Skirt

1. Referring to "Using Embroidery Stitches" on page 51, make 5 to 10 French knots in each flower center.

2. Cut a 38" x 38" square of felt for the backing. Center and pin the appliquéd top on the backing and use as a guide to cut the outside edge of the backing. With thread that matches the tree-skirt background, stipple-quilt through both layers between the outside edge of the tree skirt and the inner vine circle, or quilt as desired.

3. Referring to "Bias Binding" on page 50, cut and join enough 2½"-wide bias strips to make approximately 180" of binding. Bind the edges of the inside circle, the side opening, and the outside edge.

WINTER ROSE TABLE TOPPER

WINTER ROSE TABLE TOPPER by Pamela Mostek. A great companion to the tree skirt, this table topper will look beautiful on your table all through the winter. Try it with an arrangement of evergreen branches or a collection of candlesticks in the center.

Materials

Yardages are based on 72"-wide wool felt and 42"-wide cotton.

1⅓ yds. antique-white felt for background

½ yd. dark green felt for leaves

1⅓ yds. felt for backing

3 pieces, each 12" x 18", black felt for center ring

3 pieces, each 12" x 18", assorted red felt for roses

⅔ yd. cotton fabric for binding

Heavy thread (for machine topstitching) or pearl
    cotton (for hand embroidery)

Template plastic

Freezer paper

33" length of string

Quilter's marking pencil

Fabric glue

Assembling the Table Topper

Referring to "Preparing the Fabric" on page 6, prepare the wool felt for cutting and sewing. Use the cutting guide on page 52 and appliqué patterns on page 57.

1. Join several pieces of freezer paper to make a 36" square. Fold the square in half vertically, then in half horizontally, and mark the center. Referring to "Drawing a Circle" on page 8, make a knot in the string 17" from the marking pencil and draw a 34"-diameter circle on freezer paper.

2. Make a plastic template of cutting guide A. Place the template on the edge of the drawn circle and trace the scalloped edge. Continue moving and tracing the scalloped edge until you've gone around the circle.

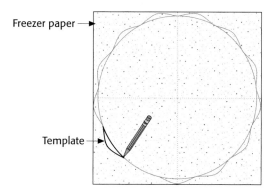

3. Cut a 38" x 38" square of white felt for the background. Iron the freezer-paper pattern to the white background and cut out along the scalloped edge.

4. Make a knot in the string 10" from the marking pencil and draw a second circle, 20" in diameter, on the white background for the inside circle.

5. Cut enough black felt strips, ½" wide, for the inside circle (approximately 70"). Place the strips around the circle, overlapping the ends as needed to complete the circle. Straight stitch along the inside and outside edges of the black strips.

6. Referring to "Adding the Appliqués" on page 8, cut and position the appliqué shapes around the black circle. Adjust the leaf-and-stem shapes slightly as needed to fit the circle. Blanket stitch around all edges except those that are layered beneath another appliqué shape.

    11 dark green leaves and stems (Template 1)

    11 assorted red roses (Template 2)

    11 dark green leaves (Template 5)

Finishing the Table Topper

1. Cut a 36" x 36" square of felt for the backing. Center and pin the appliquéd top on the backing and use it as a pattern to trace the scalloped edge. With a marking pencil, trace around the scalloped edge. Remove the appliquéd top and cut the backing on the drawn line.

2. Layer the top and the backing, matching the scalloped edges. Quilt as desired.

3. Referring to "Bias Binding" on page 50, cut and join enough 2½"-wide bias strips to make approximately 130" of binding. Bind the edges.

Placement Guide

BLOWING IN THE WIND LAP QUILT

BLOWING IN THE WIND LAP QUILT by Patti Eaton. Machine quilted by Sandra Hawks. When we combined richly colored flannel prints and wool felt, we were thrilled with the stunning results! This warm and wonderful lap quilt is perfect for snuggling up by the fire or for an eye-catching accent on your favorite chair or bed.

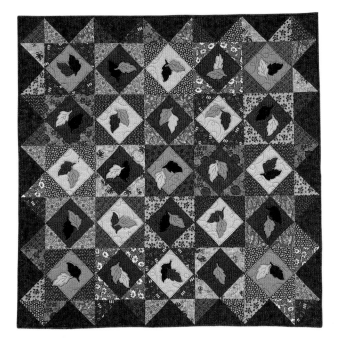

Materials

*Yardages are based on 36"-wide wool felt and
42"-wide cotton flannel.*

2¼ yds. *total* assorted burgundy print flannels

2¼ yds. *total* assorted green print flannels

¾ yd. rose felt

½ yd. light green felt

½ yd. medium green felt

1½ yds. solid burgundy flannel for border and binding

3 pieces, each 12" x 18", assorted green felt for leaves

2 pieces, each 9" x 12", assorted burgundy felt for
    leaves

3⅔ yds. cotton flannel for backing

66" x 66" piece batting

Heavy thread (for machine topstitching) or pearl
    cotton (for hand stitching)

Template plastic

Freezer paper

Quilter's marking pencil

Fabric glue

Cutting

Referring to "Preparing the Fabric" on page 6, prepare
the wool felt for cutting and sewing.

From the assorted burgundy print flannels, cut:

13 squares, each 10½" x 10½"

11 squares, each 6" x 6"

From the assorted green print flannels, cut:

12 squares, each 10½" x 10½"

11 squares, each 6" x 6"

From the rose felt, cut:

12 squares, each 6½" x 6½"

From the light green felt, cut:

8 squares, each 6½" x 6½"

From the medium green felt, cut:

5 squares, each 6½" x 6½"

From the solid burgundy flannel, cut:

4 strips, each 6"x 42"; crosscut the strips into 22
    squares, each 6" x 6"

7 strips, each 2½" x 42", for binding

Assembling the Quilt

Use the appliqué pattern on page 57.

1. Referring to "Adding the Appliqués" on page 8, cut
   a total of 49 green and burgundy leaves (Template
   6) from the wool felt. Referring to the color photo
   above left, position and straight stitch the leaves to
   the 6½" rose, light green, and medium green felt
   squares. Stitch veins on the leaves.

2. Blanket stitch a 6½" rose felt square to a 10½"
   green print flannel square. Repeat with the 6½"
   light and medium green felt squares on the 10½"
   burgundy print flannel squares.

Make 12.

Make 13.

3. Referring to the color photo on page 17, arrange the completed blocks in 5 rows of 5 blocks each, alternating burgundy and green blocks from row to row. Sew the blocks together, then join the rows.

4. To make the half-square triangle units for the border, place a 6" burgundy or green print flannel square on top of a 6" solid burgundy flannel square with right sides together. Draw a diagonal line from corner to corner on the top square. Stitch a scant ¼" on either side of the drawn line. Cut on the drawn line. Trim the squares to 5½" x 5½".

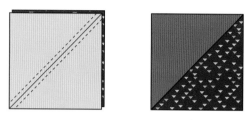

Make 44.

5. Arrange the half-square triangle units around the outside of the quilt, referring to the photo on page 17 and diagram below. Sew 10 units together for each of the side borders and add these to the sides of the quilt top. Sew 12 units together for the top and bottom borders and add these to the top and bottom edges.

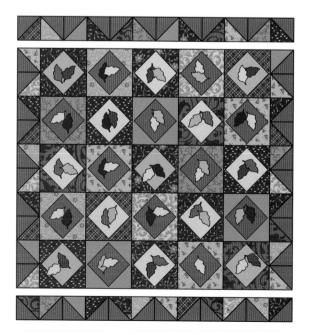

Finishing the Quilt

1. Divide the backing fabric crosswise into 2 equal panels, each approximately 66" long. Remove the selvages and join the pieces to make a single large backing panel. Layer the quilt top, batting, and backing; baste. Quilt as desired.

2. Referring to "Straight-Grain Binding" on page 50, bind the edges of the quilt.

GOLDEN PEARS TABLE RUNNER

GOLDEN PEARS TABLE RUNNER by Pamela Mostek. Inspired by traditional folk-art penny rugs, the unique, handmade look of this table runner will make it a charming accent for your winter table. We created it in shades of gold on black, but it would be gorgeous in any color scheme.

Materials

Yardages are based on 36"-wide wool felt.

⅝ yd. black for background

¾ yd. gold for tongues

4 pieces, each 9" x 12", assorted greens for leaves

6 pieces, each 9" x 12", assorted golds for pears and leaves

3 pieces, each 9" x 12", gold for small pennies

4 pieces, each 12" x 18", black for large pennies

Scrap of brown for stems

⅝ yd. for backing

Heavy thread (for machine topstitching) or pearl cotton (for hand stitching)

Template plastic

Freezer paper

Quilter's marking pencil

Fabric glue

Assembling the Table Runner

Referring to "Preparing the Fabric" on page 6, prepare the wool felt for cutting and sewing. Use the cutting guide on page 52 and appliqué patterns on pages 57–58.

1. Cut a 12" x 28" piece of black for the background. Mark the center on each of the 12" ends.

2. Make a plastic template of cutting guide B; be sure to indicate the center point on the template. Matching the center point of the template with the center mark on the end of the felt, trace along the curved edge with a marking pencil.

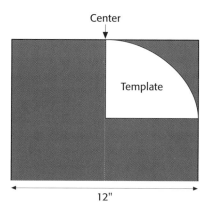

3. Flip the template to the other side, match the centers, and trace along the curved edge. Cut out the curve on the drawn line. Repeat for the other end of the 12" x 28" black background.

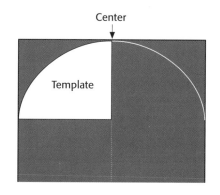

4. Referring to "Adding the Appliqués" on page 8, cut and position the appliqué shapes as shown. Blanket stitch around all edges except those that are layered beneath another appliqué shape.

> 14 small assorted green leaves (Template 7)
>
> 8 large assorted gold and green leaves (Template 8)
>
> 4 brown stems (Template 9)
>
> 4 assorted gold pears (Template 10)
>
> 2 gold pear centers (Template 11)

Placement Guide

Adding the Tongues

1. Make plastic templates of the tongue (Template 12), large penny (Template 13), and small penny (Template 14). Using the freezer-paper method, trace and cut out 22 gold tongues, 22 large black pennies, and 22 small gold pennies. Layer a large and a small penny on top of a tongue, glue in place, and blanket stitch around the edges of the pennies. Make 22 tongues.

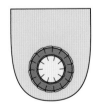

2. For the tongue backings, cut four 3½"-wide strips from the gold wool. Position the tongues on the strips and blanket stitch along the rounded edges, leaving the straight edges unstitched. Trim the backing ⅛" from the appliquéd tongues.

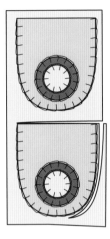

Finishing the Table Runner

1. Cut a 12" x 28" piece of felt for backing. Center and pin the appliquéd table runner on the backing. Place the 22 tongues evenly around the edge of the table runner, inserting the unstitched ends about ½" between the top and backing. Pin the tongues in place.

2. Blanket stitch around the edge of the table runner through all layers: table-runner top, the inserted tongue edges, and the backing.

3. From the underside, trim the backing next to the stitching line and from behind the tongues, being careful not to cut through the stitching or the tongues.

POINSETTIAS

POINSETTIA GREETINGS WALL HANGING AND POINSETTIA MANTEL COVER by Patti Eaton.
Welcome your holiday guests with these festive poinsettia quilts in traditional Christmas colors.
We love to place the wall hanging above a mantel decorated for the holidays, but it would be perfect in an
entryway, too. You can make the mantel cover a perfect fit for your own home by simply enlarging
or reducing the paper patterns as needed.

POINSETTIA GREETINGS WALL HANGING

Finished Size: 41" x 16"

Materials

Yardages are based on 36"-wide wool felt.

1½ yds. dark green for border

1½ yds. cream for background and backing

½ yd. dark red for letters and petals

1 piece, 12" x 18", of bright red for petals

⅓ yd. light green for leaves and vines

Scrap of gold for poinsettia centers and pennies

Heavy thread (for machine topstitching) or pearl
  cotton (for hand stitching)

Template plastic

Freezer paper

Quilter's marking pencil

Fabric glue

Pinking shears or rotary wave blade

Wooden dowel for hanging

Assembling the Wall Hanging

Referring to "Preparing the Fabric" on page 6, prepare the wool felt for cutting and sewing. Use the cutting guide on page 52 and appliqué patterns on pages 57–58.

1. To make a cutting template for the scalloped center section, cut a 16" x 41" piece of freezer paper and fold it in half vertically and then in half horizontally to mark the centers. Unfold the paper, and with a long ruler and a pencil, mark a 3¼"-wide border around the outside edge.

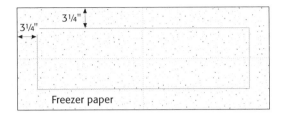

2. Make a plastic template of cutting guide C. Beginning in the center on the long sides, align one edge of the template with the vertical center crease on the paper, and the bottom of the template with the edge of the paper. With a marking pencil, trace the curved edge of the template and make a small mark along the right edge to indicate where to align the template next. Move the template, aligning the edge to the mark, and trace the next curve. Continue moving the template and tracing the curves. Repeat the scallops on the left half of the paper. Repeat the scallops along the opposite long edge of the paper. Redraw the ends of the curves at each end to round them a bit, then connect the top and bottom curves with a straight line. Cut out the center of the paper on the curved lines.

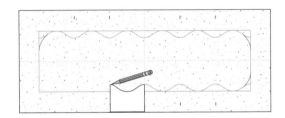

3. Cut a 16" x 41" piece of dark green felt for the border. Iron the paper pattern to the felt. Trace the inner curved edges on the felt. Cut out the center portion of the felt on the curved lines.

4. Cut a 14" x 37" piece of cream felt for the background. Center and pin the green border on top of the cream rectangle. Blanket stitch around the inside edge of the green border.

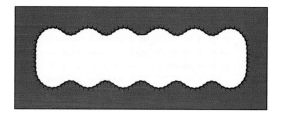

5. Referring to "Adding the Appliqués" on page 8, cut and position the appliqué shapes as shown. Blanket stitch around the edges of the letters and pennies. Straight stitch around remaining appliqués except those that are layered beneath another shape. Stitch veins on the leaves.

    7 large green leaves (Template 6)
    4 small green leaves (Template 15)
    14 large assorted red petals (Template 15)
    7 small assorted red petals (Template 16)
    1 small light green petal (Template 16)
    1 small gold petal (Template 16)
    2 gold centers (Template 17)

    3 large gold pennies (Template 4)
    7 small gold pennies (Template 14)
    7 green stems, each ⅜" x 6"
    All red letters in GREETINGS

Finishing the Wall Hanging

1. Cut a 17" x 42" piece of cream felt for the backing. Center the appliquéd top on the backing. Blanket stitch across the top, starting and stopping at each end. Beginning 1½" from the top edge, blanket stitch down the side, across the bottom, and up the other side, stopping 1½" from the top edge. This forms a pocket for the dowel. With pinking shears or a rotary wave blade, trim the backing ⅛" from the stitched appliquéd top.

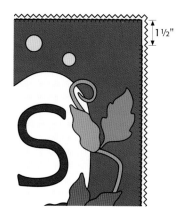

2. To hang, insert the wooden dowel in the pocket.

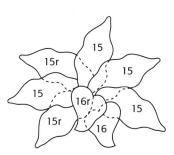

Upper-Left Poinsettia   Lower-Right Poinsettia

Placement Guide

POINSETTIA MANTEL COVER

Finished Size: 48" x 18"

Materials

Yardages are based on 36"-wide wool felt.

1¾ yds. green for top

1¾ yds. cream for trim and backing

⅓ yd. red for petals

⅓ yd. green for leaves and stems

1 piece, 9" x 12", gold for poinsettia center and pennies

Heavy thread (for machine topstitching) or pearl cotton (for hand stitching)

Template plastic

Freezer paper

Quilter's marking pencil

Fabric glue

Basting spray

Pinking shears or rotary wave blade (optional)

Assembling the Mantel Cover

Referring to "Preparing the Fabric" on page 6, prepare the wool felt for cutting and sewing. Use the cutting guides on pages 53–55 and appliqué patterns on pages 57–58.

1. To make a cutting template for the scalloped edge, cut a piece of freezer paper 18" x 48" and fold it in half vertically and then in half horizontally.

2. Make plastic templates of cutting guides D-1, D-2, D-3, and D-4 (sections 1, 2, 3, and 4). Beginning in the center on the long side, place sections 1, 2, 3, and 4 next to each other on the paper and trace the scalloped edge. Repeat for the other side, reversing the patterns. Cut the scalloped edge on the drawn line.

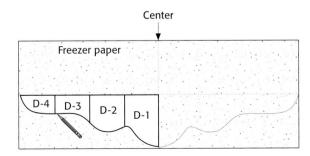

Center

Freezer paper

D-4 | D-3 | D-2 | D-1

TIP Reduce or enlarge sections 1, 2, 3, and 4 as needed if your mantel is longer or shorter than 48".

3. Cut an 18" x 48" piece of green felt for the top. Iron the freezer-paper pattern to the green felt and cut along the scalloped edge.

4. Referring to "Adding the Appliqués" on page 8, cut and position the 1¾"-wide cream strips along the sides and bottom, overlapping them as needed. Straight stitch along both edges of the strips; then cut and position the remaining appliqué shapes. Straight stitch around all edges except those that are layered beneath another appliqué shape. Stitch veins on the leaves.

> 4 cream strips, each ¾" x 18" (cut with pinking shears or wave blade)
>
> 6 green stems, each ⅜" x 9"
>
> 12 large red petals (Template 15)
>
> 10 small red petals (Template 16)
>
> 1 gold poinsettia center (Template 17)
>
> 8 large green leaves (Template 6)
>
> 4 small green leaves (Template 15)
>
> 5 large gold pennies (Template 13)
>
> 8 small gold pennies (Template 14)

Placement Guide

Finishing the Mantel Cover

Cut a 19" x 49" piece of cream felt for the backing. Lightly cover it with basting spray. Center and pin the appliquéd top on the backing. Blanket stitch around the outside edge. Trim the backing ⅛" from the stitched appliquéd top. Use pinking shears or a rotary wave blade if desired.

SNOWBIRDS TABLE RUNNER

SNOWBIRDS TABLE RUNNER by Patti Eaton. What could be simpler—or more eye-catching? This easy-to-create table runner will look wonderful in your home all winter if you make it in our soft shades of tans and creams on a brown background. Or try it in traditional reds and greens, and it will be perfect for the holiday season.

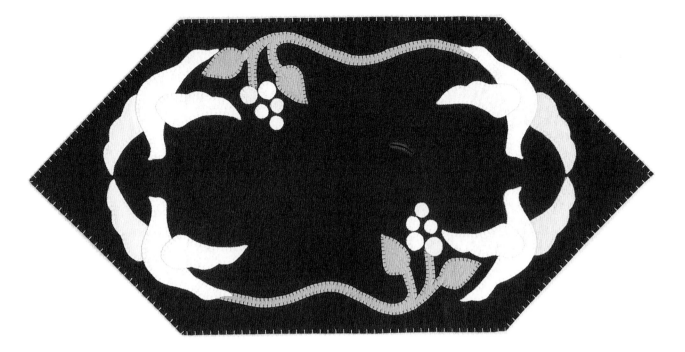

Materials

Yardages are based on 36"-wide wool felt.

1¼ yds. brown for background

1¼ yds. cream for backing and bird wings

⅓ yd. white for birds and berries

⅓ yd. tan for leaves and stems

Heavy thread (for machine topstitching) or pearl cotton (for hand stitching)

Template plastic

Quilter's marking pencil

Fabric glue

Pinking shears or rotary wave blade (optional)

Assembling the Table Runner

Referring to "Preparing the Fabric" on page 6, prepare the wool felt for cutting and sewing. Use the appliqué patterns on pages 57–58.

1. Cut an 18" x 36" piece of brown felt for the background. Mark the center of each 18" end. Measure 8" from each of the 4 corners along the 36" side and make a mark. Draw diagonal lines from the center mark on the ends to the 8" marks as shown.

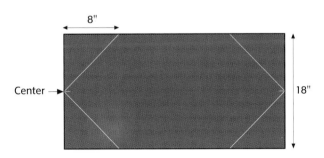

2. With a quilting ruler and a rotary cutter, cut on the drawn lines.

3. Referring to "Adding the Appliqués" on page 8, cut and position the appliqué shapes as shown. Blanket stitch around all edges except those that are layered beneath another appliqué shape.

  4 white wings (Template 18)

  4 cream wings (Template 18)

  4 white snowbirds (Template 19)

  4 large white berries (Template 4)

  6 small white berries (Template 14)

  2 tan leaves and stems (Template 1), adding
     9" to the length of the stem

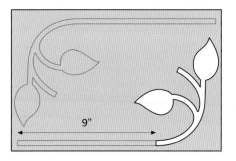

Finishing the Table Runner

Cut a 19" x 37" piece of cream felt for the backing. Center and pin the appliquéd top on the backing. Blanket stitch around the edge of the appliquéd top. Trim the backing ¼" from the appliquéd top, using pinking shears or a rotary wave blade if desired.

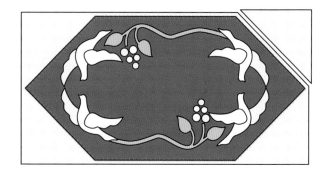

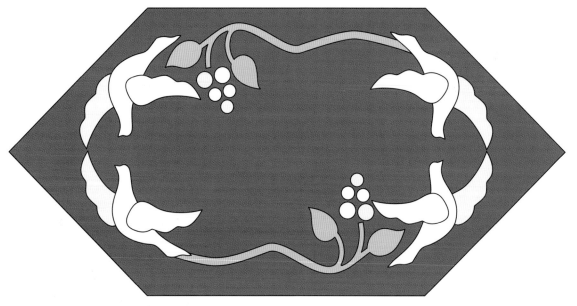

Placement Guide

NUTS AND BERRIES PILLOW

NUTS AND BERRIES PILLOW by Pamela Mostek. We love pillows created in wool felt!
A quick-and-easy accent for your living room or bedroom, pillows add a touch of personality in a very short time!
This pillow of nuts and berries will look wonderful in the autumn and all through the winter.

Materials

Yardages are based on 36"-wide wool felt.

¾ yd. tan for inner background and backing

⅔ yd. dark red for middle background and berries

⅔ yd. black for outer background

3 pieces, each 9" x 12", assorted greens for leaves and vine circle

1 piece, 9" x 12", gold for leaves

Scraps of brown and dark brown for acorns

Heavy thread (for machine topstitching) or pearl cotton (for hand stitching)

Template plastic

Freezer paper

12" length of string

Quilter's marking pencil

Fabric glue

Soup bowl for corner template

Pinking shears

Fiberfill stuffing

Assembling the Pillow

Referring to "Preparing the Fabric" on page 6, prepare the wool felt for cutting and sewing. Use the appliqué patterns on pages 57–58.

1. Cut a 13" x 13" square of tan felt for the inner background. Fold the square in half vertically, then in half horizontally, and mark the center. Referring to "Drawing a Circle" on page 8, make a knot in the string 5" from the marking pencil and draw a 10"-diameter circle. This will be a placement guide for the vine and leaves.

2. Cut enough ¼"-wide green strips to make the vine circle (approximately 36"). Place the strips around the circle, overlapping the ends as needed to complete the circle. Stitch through the center of the green strips.

3. Referring to "Adding the Appliqués" on page 8, cut and position the appliqué shapes around the circle as shown. Straight stitch around all edges except those that are layered beneath another appliqué shape. Stitch veins on the leaves as shown in photo above left.

    26 assorted green and gold leaves (Template 7)

    4 brown acorns (Template 20)

    4 dark brown acorn caps (Template 21)

    8 red berries (Template 14)

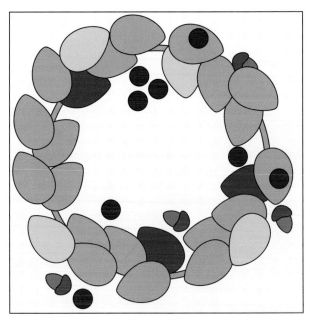

Placement Guide

4. With a marking pencil, draw tendrils that wrap around the wreath. Referring to "Using Embroidery Stitches" on page 51, stem stitch the tendrils.

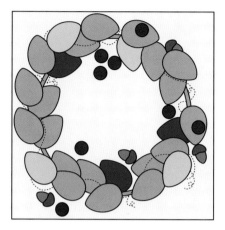

5. To make curved corners on the tan background, position a soup bowl in the corner and trace the curve with a marking pencil. Repeat for all corners and cut on the drawn line.

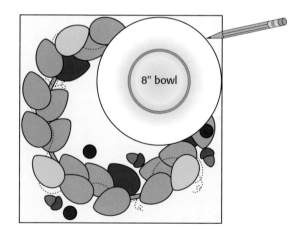

6. Cut a 15" x 15" square of red felt for the middle background. Center and pin the appliquéd top on the red square, and blanket stitch around the edge of the pillow top. Use a long ruler and a rotary cutter to square up the corners of the red square in case it stretched during handling.

7. Cut a 17" x 17" square of black felt for the outer background. Center and pin the pillow top on the black square, and blanket stitch around the edge of the pillow top. Square up the corners, if necessary, to complete the pillow top.

Finishing the Pillow

1. Cut a 19" x 19" square of tan felt for the backing. Center and pin the pillow top on the backing. Using the edge of the black border as a guide, machine topstitch through all layers ½" from the edge around all sides, leaving a 6" opening.

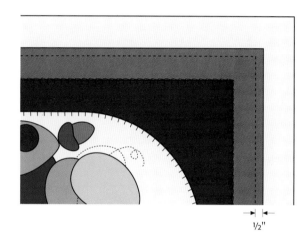

2. With pinking shears, trim the black background to ¼" from the stitching; trim the tan backing ¼" from the black background.

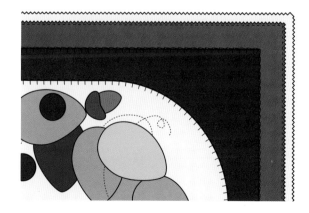

3. Stuff lightly with fiberfill. Machine stitch the opening closed.

AMERICAN BEAUTY LAP QUILT

AMERICAN BEAUTY LAP QUILT by Patti Eaton. Machine quilted by Sandra Hawks. Wintertime blossoms entwined with leaves and vines create a beautiful center medallion in this soft and cozy flannel lap quilt. We think the softly shaded print of the flannel is a perfect complement to the blanket-stitched appliqués of wool felt.

Finished Size: 58" x 72"

Materials

Yardages are based on 36"-wide wool felt and 42"-wide cotton flannel.

2¾ yds. floral-print flannel for quilt, outer border, and binding

1⅔ yds. *total* assorted light-colored flannels for appliqué squares and accent borders

⅓ yd. light purple flannel for accent borders

⅓ yd. light green flannel for accent borders

⅓ yd. dark green flannel for inner border

½ yd. light green felt for stems and leaves

¼ yd. purple heather felt for roses

¼ yd. dark green felt for ring, leaves, and berries

Scraps of gold felt for flower centers

4½ yds. cotton flannel for backing

63" x 78" piece of batting

Heavy thread (for machine topstitching) or pearl cotton (for hand stitching)

Template plastic

Freezer paper

15" length of string

Quilter's marking pencil

Fabric glue

Cutting

Referring to "Preparing the Fabric" on page 6, prepare the wool felt for cutting and sewing.

From the floral print flannel, cut:

2 squares, each 21⅞" x 21⅞"; cut squares once diagonally to yield 4 triangles

7 strips, each 7½" x 42"

7 strips, each 2½" x 42"

From the assorted light colored flannels, cut:

9 squares, each 10⅜" x 10⅜"

6 squares, each 8" x 8"

From the light purple flannel, cut:

1 strip, 8⅜" x 42"; crosscut into 3 squares, each 8⅜" x 8⅜"

From the light green flannel, cut:

1 strip, 8⅜" x 42"; crosscut into 3 squares, each 8⅜" x 8⅜"

From the dark green flannel, cut:

6 strips, 1½ " x 42

Assembling the Quilt Top

Use the appliqué patterns on pages 57–58.

1. Sew the 9 light 10⅜" blocks into 3 rows of 3 blocks each. Join the rows.

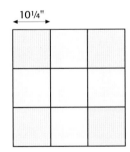

10¼"

2. Cut a 15" x 15" square of freezer paper. Referring to "Drawing a Circle" on page 8, make a knot on the string 7¼" from the marking pencil, and draw a 14½"-diameter circle on the freezer paper. Cut out the circle.

3. Iron the freezer-paper pattern to the center of the flannel squares. Cut 4 strips, each ½" x 11½", from the dark green felt. Place the strips around the edge of the paper circle and pin or glue in place. Remove the paper pattern.

4. Referring to "Adding the Appliqués" on page 8, cut and position the appliqué shapes around the circle. Blanket stitch around all edges except those that are layered beneath another appliqué shape.

    13 dark green leaves (Template 15)

    12 large dark green berries (Template 4)

    8 light green leaves and stems (Template 1)

    13 purple roses (Template 2)

    13 gold flower centers (Template 4)

Placement Guide

TIP After positioning the circle, leaves, and flowers, begin stitching along the inner edge of the circle, carefully lifting flowers and leaves as you come to them so that you can stitch the circle underneath. Repeat for the outer edge of the circle.

5. Add the floral print triangles to each side of the appliquéd square. The unit should measure 42½" x 42½", including seam allowances.

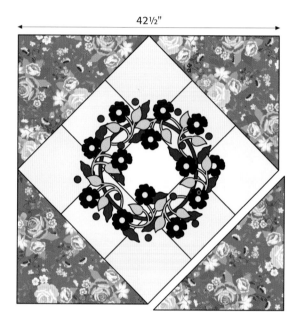

42½"

6. With right sides together, layer a purple 8⅜" square and a light green 8⅜" square. Draw a diagonal line on the wrong side of the top fabric. Stitch a scant ¼" on either side of the line. Cut on the drawn line and press.

Make 6.   Cut.

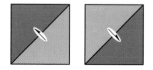

7. With right sides together, layer an 8" half-square triangle unit on top of an 8" light square. Draw a diagonal line from corner to corner and stitch a scant ¼" on either side of the line. Cut on the drawn line and press. Trim the squares to 7½" x 7½".

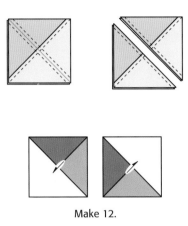

Make 12.

8. Referring to the color photo on page 33 and the diagram below, join 6 units each to make 2 strips for the top and bottom of the quilt top. Sew these to the top and bottom edges.

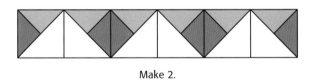

Make 2.

Adding the Borders

1. Sew the 1½"-wide inner border strips together end to end. Measure the quilt through the center vertically, and cut 2 strips for the side borders. Mark the centers on the sides of the quilt and the border strips. With right sides together and matching centers and ends, sew the side borders to the quilt top.

2. Measure the quilt through the center horizontally, including the borders you just added. Mark the centers and sew the strips to the top and bottom edges, matching the centers and ends.

3. Repeat steps 1 and 2 with the 7½"-wide outer border strips.

Finishing the Quilt

1. Divide the backing fabric crosswise into 2 equal panels, each approximately 81" long. Remove the selvages and join the pieces to make a single large backing. Layer the quilt top, batting, and backing; baste. Quilt as desired.

2. Referring to "Straight-Grain Binding" on page 50, bind the edges of the quilt.

WARM WELCOME WREATH WALL HANGING

WARM WELCOME WREATH WALL HANGING by Pamela Mostek. Winter fruits, nuts, and berries highlight this wreath of blanket-stitched appliqué. We created it in deep, harvest tones so that it would be a perfect accent for the fall season too.

Materials

Yardages are based on 36"-wide wool felt.

1½ yds. black for background, berries, and backing

¾ yd. burgundy for border, tabs, and berries

4 pieces, each 12" x 18", assorted greens for leaves

1 piece, 9" x 12", gold for pears

1 piece, 9" x 12", red for apple

Scrap of brown for stems and acorn caps

Scrap of tan for acorns

Heavy thread (for machine topstitching) or pearl cotton (for hand stitching)

Template plastic

Freezer paper

12" length of string

Quilter's marking pencil

Fabric glue

Pinking shears or rotary wave blade

24" wooden dowel or branch for hanging

Cutting

Referring to "Preparing the Fabric" on page 6, prepare the wool felt for cutting and sewing.

From the black felt, cut:

1 square, 15" x 15"

1 square, 18" x 18"

4 rectangles, each 3½" x 5"

From the burgundy felt, cut:

1 square, 18" x 18"

4 rectangles, each 2½" x 5"

Assembling the Wall Hanging

Use the appliqué patterns on pages 57–59.

1. Referring to "Drawing a Circle" on page 8, make the knot in the string 5½" from the marking pencil and draw an 11"-diameter circle on the 15" black square. This will be a guide for positioning the fruits and leaves.

2. Referring to "Adding the Appliqués" on page 8, cut and position the appliqué shapes around the circle, leaving an opening at the top of the circle. Blanket stitch around all edges except those that are layered beneath another appliqué shape.

17 assorted green leaves (Template 7)

5 assorted green leaves (Template 8)

2 gold pears (Template 10)

1 red apple (Template 22)

3 brown stems (Template 9)

5 tan acorns (Template 20)

5 brown acorn caps (Template 21)

8 small burgundy berries (Template 14)

Placement Guide

3. On the black background square, measure 2" from each corner and make a mark. Draw a diagonal line connecting the marks, and cut off the corner, using a ruler and rotary cutter.

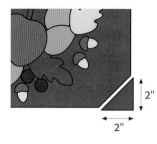

4. Center and pin the appliquéd background on the 18" burgundy square. Blanket stitch around the edges of the appliquéd top. Trim the burgundy square to 17" x 17".

5. Center a 2½" x 5" burgundy tab on top of a 3½" x 5" black tab backing. Blanket stitch both long edges. Make 4 tabs. With pinking shears or a rotary wave blade, trim the black backing ⅛" from the stitching.

Make 4.

6. Fold the tabs in half lengthwise. Position them on the wrong side of the burgundy square, spacing them evenly across the top. The ends should be about ½" below the edge of the square. Pin the tabs securely in place.

Finishing the Wall Hanging

1. Position and pin the appliquéd top and tabs on the 18" black backing square. Blanket stitch around the edges of the appliquéd top. Trim the backing ⅛" from the stitched appliquéd top, using pinking shears or a rotary wave blade if desired.

2. To hang, insert a wooden dowel or branch through the tabs.

MIDAS TOUCH WALL HANGING

MIDAS TOUCH WALL HANGING by Patti Eaton. We added the unexpected glitz of gold metallic thread
to wool felt and were very pleased with the effect. For even more holiday glow, we
combined the wool felt with a cotton metallic print.

Materials

Yardages are based on 36"-wide wool felt and
42"-wide cotton.

1½ yds. tan felt for outer border and backing

⅔ yd. cream felt for inner border

½ yd. metallic print cotton for appliqué background

3 pieces, each 9" x 12", assorted gold felt for appliqués

1 piece, 9" x 12", copper felt for leaves and flower center

1 piece, 9" x 12", white felt for wings, birds, and petals

1 piece, 9" x 12", cream felt for leaves, petals, and wings

17" x 18" piece of thin batting

Gold heavy thread (for machine topstitching) or pearl cotton (for hand stitching)

Template plastic

Freezer paper

20" length of string

Quilter's marking pencil

Fabric glue

Basting spray

Pinking shears or rotary wave blade

2 small plastic curtain rings for hanging

Making the Border Pattern

Referring to "Preparing the Fabric" on page 6, prepare the wool felt for cutting and sewing.

1. To make a border pattern, cut an 18" x 20" piece of freezer paper. Fold the paper in half lengthwise to mark the center.

2. With a long ruler and a pencil, draw a line 2" from the edge on all sides. Now draw a second line 2½" from the outside edge.

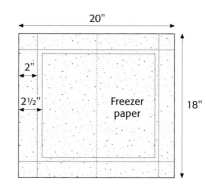

3. Tie a piece of string to a marking pencil. Place the pencil at the center of the 2" line at the top edge. Hold the string taut about 12" from the pencil and slowly draw an arc from the left margin to the right margin. This will be the cutting line for the outer border pattern.

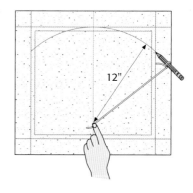

Assembling the Wall Hanging

Use the appliqué patterns on pages 57–58.

1. Cut an 18" x 20" piece of tan felt for the outer border. Iron the freezer-paper pattern to the piece of tan felt. Cut away the center section on the 2" drawn lines, remembering to cut on the outside arc line. Reserve the center section of the paper pattern for step 3.

2. Cut a 19" x 21" piece of cream felt for the inner border. Center the 18" x 20" tan outer border on top of the 19" x 21" piece of cream felt. Blanket stitch the inside edge of the tan border to the cream felt.

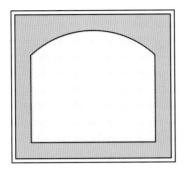

3. Using the center section of the paper pattern from step 1, a ruler, and a pencil, mark a second arc ½" from the first one. Center and iron the pattern to the cream felt. Cut the center of the pattern and cream felt on the 2½" drawn lines and the second arc line.

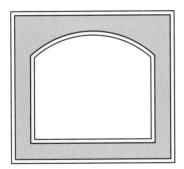

4. Cut a 17" x 18" piece from the metallic print cotton for the appliqué background. Spray baste one side of the batting piece and press it to the wrong side of the cotton print.

5. Center and pin the outer and inner border unit on top of the cotton print. Blanket stitch the cotton print to the edge of the inner border.

6. Referring to "Adding the Appliqués" on page 8, cut and position the appliqué shapes on the cotton print, with some pieces overlapping the borders. Straight stitch around all edges except those that are layered beneath another appliqué shape. Stitch veins on the leaves.

    10 assorted cream, gold, and copper leaves (Template 6)

    2 white wings (Template 18)

    2 cream wings (Template 18)

    2 white birds (Template 19)

    8 large cream, white, and gold petals (Template 15)

    2 small white and cream petals (Template 16)

    1 copper flower center (Template 17)

Placement Guide

Finishing the Wall Hanging

1. Cut a 20" x 22" piece of tan felt for the backing. Center the appliquéd top on the backing and pin. Blanket stitch around the outer edge of the tan border, through the cream border and backing. With pinking shears, trim the cream border and tan backing ¼" from the stitched appliquéd top.

2. Hand sew 2 small plastic rings to the top corners on the back for hanging.

WINTER BLUES

WINTER BLUES WALL HANGING AND SNOWFLAKE PILLOW by Pamela Mostek. The blue, appliquéd snowflakes look almost like trapunto in this striking Four Patch wall hanging. To "pop" the blue snowflakes up even more, we stipple quilted behind them with silver metallic thread. The white, reverse appliquéd snowflakes add to the rich, layered look of this icy-blue wintertime wall hanging. For a coordinated look, try the easy-to-make pillow.

WINTER BLUES WALL HANGING

Finished Size: 22" x 22"

Materials

*Yardages are based on 36"-wide wool felt and
42"-wide cotton.*

¾ yd. dark blue felt for inner border

1⅝ yds. medium blue felt for snowflakes, block
    backgrounds, and outer border

⅔ yd. white felt for block backgrounds

1 yd. felt for backing

⅔ yd. cotton print for binding

Heavy thread (for machine topstitching) in blue and
    white or pearl cotton (for hand stitching)

Silver metallic thread for quilting

Template plastic

Freezer paper

Quilter's marking pencil

Basting spray

2 small plastic curtain rings for hanging

Cutting

Referring to "Preparing the Fabric" on page 6, prepare
the wool felt for cutting and sewing.

From the dark blue felt, cut:

    1 square, 18" x 18"

From the medium blue felt, cut:

    1 square, 22" x 22"

    4 squares, each 8" x 8"

From the white felt, cut:

    1 square, 16" x 16"

From the felt for backing, cut:

    1 square, 22" x 22"

Assembling the Wall Hanging

Use the appliqué template on page 59.

1. Spray baste the back of the 18" dark blue square.
   Center the square on the 22" medium blue square.
   Blanket stitch around the edge of the dark blue
   square.

2. Spray baste the back of the 16" white square. Center
   the white square on the dark blue square.

3. Referring to "Adding the Appliqués" on page 8,
   make a plastic template or freezer-paper template of
   the snowflake pattern (Template 23). Trace the pattern onto freezer paper and iron the paper onto 2 of
   the 8" medium blue squares. Starting along a line
   within the pattern and not on the outside edge,
   carefully cut out the snowflake, reserving the outer
   portion and inner circle for reverse appliqué.

4. Spray baste the reverse-appliqué blue snowflake
   background and the blue center. Align the straight
   edges of the blue background with the edges of the
   white square; center the blue circle on the same
   white square. Repeat with the second reverse-
   appliqué snowflake on the opposite corner of the

white square. With blue thread, blanket stitch around the edges of the reverse-appliqué snowflake and the inner edges of the blue squares.

5. Iron the snowflake pattern on the 2 remaining 8" medium blue squares. Cut out the blue snowflakes.

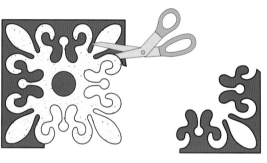

Discard.

6. Spray baste a blue snowflake and center it on one of the white areas. Repeat with the second blue snowflake on the opposite corner of the white square. With blue thread, blanket stitch around the edges of the snowflakes.

7. With white thread, blanket stitch around the outside edges of the white-and-blue squares.

Finishing the Wall Hanging

1. Position and pin the appliquéd top on the 22" square of backing. With metallic thread, stipple-quilt on the white snowflakes, the white background of the blue snowflakes, and the outer border.

2. Measure the outside dimensions of the appliquéd wall hanging. Because of layering, blanket stitching, and quilting, the dimensions may vary slightly from 22" square. Cut a piece of freezer paper to match the dimensions of your wall hanging.

3. Make a plastic template of cutting guide E on page 56. Place the template in one corner, and draw the scalloped corner on the paper square. Repeat for the remaining 3 corners. Move the template along each side and trace the scalloped edges. You may have to slightly adjust the scallops as you move around the square to get them to come out evenly. It all depends on the actual size of your wall hanging.

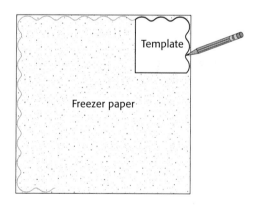

Template

Freezer paper

4. Iron the freezer-paper pattern to the backing. Cut out the scalloped edge through all layers—the backing and the appliquéd top.

5. Referring to "Bias Binding" on page 50, cut enough 2½"-wide bias strips to make approximately 100" of binding. Sew the binding to the edges of the wall hanging.

6. Hand sew 2 small plastic rings to the top corners on the back for hanging.

SNOWFLAKE PILLOW

Finished Size: 13" x 13"

Materials

Yardages are based on 36"-wide wool felt.

½ yd. dark blue for border

½ yd. white for snowflake and backing

1 piece, 9" x 12", light blue for Four Patch block

1 piece, 9" x 12", light green for Four Patch block

Heavy thread (for machine topstitching) or pearl
cotton (for hand stitching)

Quilter's marking pencil

Basting spray

Fiberfill stuffing

Cutting

Referring to "Preparing the Fabric" on page 6, prepare
the wool felt for cutting and sewing.

From the dark blue felt, cut:

1 square, 13" x 13"

From the white felt, cut:

1 square, 8" x 8"

1 square, 15" x 15"

From the light blue felt, cut:

2 squares, each 5" x 5"

From the light green felt, cut:

2 squares, each 5" x 5"

Assembling the Pillow

Use the appliqué pattern on page 59.

1. Using a ⅜"-wide seam allowance, sew each 5" light
   blue square to a 5" light green square. Press the
   seams open. Sew the pairs together to make a Four
   Patch block for the background. Press the seams
   open.

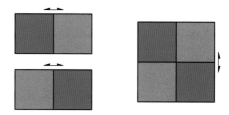

2. Center the Four Patch block on the 13" dark blue
   square. Blanket stitch all around the edges of the
   Four Patch block.

3. Referring to "Adding the Appliqués" on page 8, cut
   1 snowflake (Template 23) from white wool. Spray
   baste the back of the snowflake and center it on the
   Four Patch block. Blanket stitch around the edges of
   the snowflake.

Finishing the Pillow

1. Center the appliquéd pillow top on the 15" white
   backing square. Using the edge of the dark blue border as a stitching guide, machine stitch ¼" from the
   edge around all sides, leaving a 5" opening for stuffing. Trim the backing ¼" from the edge of the dark
   blue border on the pillow top.

Stitch ¼" from edge.
Trim to ¼" from
border edge.

2. Stuff lightly with fiberfill and machine stitch the
   opening closed.

ROSE RIBBON PILLOW

ROSE RIBBON PILLOW by Pamela Mostek. If you love touches of embroidery, this project is for you!
We've added green embroidered vines to this very elegant decorator pillow. The "lace" background
behind the appliquéd roses gives it a delicate, one-of-a-kind look.

Materials

Yardages are based on 36"-wide wool felt.

⅔ yd. black for background and backing

¼ yd. white for lace

⅛ yd. dark green for vine

1 piece, 12" x 18", light green for leaves and stems

1 piece, 9" x 12", dark pink for rose

1 piece, 9" x 12", burgundy for rose

Heavy thread (for machine topstitching)

White and green pearl cotton (for hand stitching)

Template plastic

Freezer paper

Quilter's marking pencil

Fabric glue

Fiberfill stuffing

Assembling the Pillow

Referring to "Preparing the Fabric" on page 6, prepare the wool felt for cutting and sewing. Use the cutting guides on page 56 and appliqué patterns on page 57.

1. To make a paper template for cutting the lace appliqué, cut a 6" x 14½" piece of freezer paper. Make plastic templates of cutting guides F and G. Place the scallop template (F) ¼" from one end, with the curve at the top of the long edge, and trace the curve. Move the template and trace the curve. Repeat 2 more times. Place the scallop-opening template (G) about ½" below each scallop and trace. Repeat on the other long side.

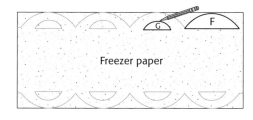

2. Cut a 6" x 14½" piece from white felt. Iron the freezer-paper template to the white felt. Cut out the scallops along both edges; cut out the opening in each scallop.

3. Cut a 10½" x 14½" piece from black felt for the background. Center the white scalloped lace on top of the black background, and blanket stitch around the top and bottom edges and the scallop openings.

4. Referring to "Adding the Appliqués" on page 8, cut and position the dark green strip on the lace first, slightly curving it as shown. Then cut and position the remaining appliqué shapes, tucking the ends of the stems under the vine. Blanket stitch around all edges except those that are layered beneath another appliqué shape.

    1 dark green strip, ½" x 15½", for vine

    2 light green leaves and stems (Template 1)

    1 burgundy rose (Template 2)

    1 dark pink rose (Template 2)

    2 black flower centers (Template 3)

Placement Guide

Finishing the Pillow

1. Referring to "Embroidery Stitches" on page 51, add white and green French knots to the flower centers.

2. With a marking pencil, draw a line for the tendrils, referring to the color photo. The tendrils should wrap around the dark green vine, with several ends wrapping around the light green stems. With a stem stitch, embroider the tendrils.

3. Cut a 10½" x 14½" piece of black felt for the backing. Position it on the appliquéd pillow top. Stitch all around the edges with a ¼"-wide seam, leaving a 5" opening on one side for turning.

4. Turn the appliquéd top to the outside out and press lightly. Stuff lightly with fiberfill and hand stitch the opening closed.

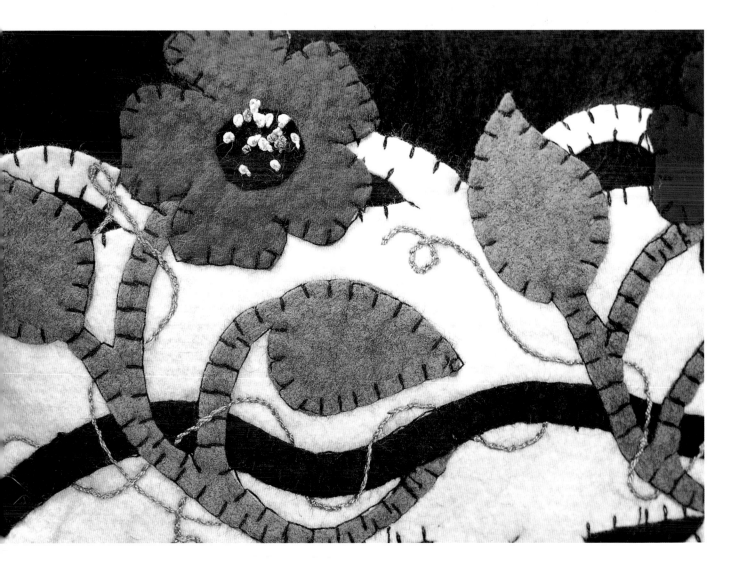

QUILTING BASICS

To assist you in creating a project that you'll be pleased with and proud of, we've included the information you'll need to complete the quilting steps in the book. Combining a few quilting techniques with wool felt is a great way to create unique, eye-catching results. We've added touches like quilting, cotton bindings, and reverse appliqué to some of the designs in this book, and we encourage you to experiment and add a sprinkling of quilting touches to any of the projects you create.

Following are a few tips to keep in mind when you combine cotton and wool felt to make your project:

❖ Select high-quality, 100 percent–cotton fabrics because they are easy to handle and durable.

❖ Prewash and dry all cotton fabrics, especially when working with flannel.

❖ Use a rotary cutter and see-through ruler for quick and easy rotary cutting.

❖ Use a standard ¼"-wide seam allowance when piecing.

❖ Always press after completing each step when working with cotton fabric.

LAYERING

Cut and piece the backing fabric so that it is at least 3" larger than the quilt top on all sides. Make a quilt sandwich by layering the backing with the wrong side up, the batting, and the quilt top with the right side up. Baste using safety pins or thread.

QUILTING

Today, many of us indulge ourselves by having our quilts professionally machine quilted. However, if you choose to either hand quilt or machine quilt a project yourself, there are many excellent references to help you. See "References" on page 62.

Smaller projects can easily be quilted on your own sewing machine. For quilting straight lines, a walking foot is very helpful. For curved designs, such as stippling, you'll need a darning foot and the ability to lower the feed dogs. This is called free-motion quilting. Refer to your machine's manual for how-tos that are unique to your particular model. When the feed dogs are lowered, the stitch length is determined by how fast you run the machine and feed the fabric under the foot. The goal is to keep the length of the stitches even. It's a good idea to practice this technique on a sample piece before quilting your project.

When stipple quilting, many quilters try not to cross a line that has already been stitched. You can make the pattern as large or as small as you wish, but circles and curves about ½" in height or width work well in most areas. Stipple quilting is a great way to fill in background areas.

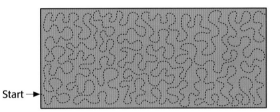

Start →

BINDING

Binding can be cut on the straight grain of the fabric or on the bias grain. If the project has curved edges, the binding strips must be cut on the bias grain so that they will bend easily around the curves. Strips for binding are cut 2½" wide. You'll need enough binding to go around the outside of the quilt plus about 10" for seams and mitered corners. The directions for each project will tell you which type of binding to use and how many strips to cut.

Straight-Grain Binding

1. Fold the fabric with selvages together and cut the required number of 2½"-wide strips across the width of the fabric.

2. Join binding strips at right angles, right sides together, and stitch from corner to corner. Trim excess fabric and press seams open.

3. Cut one end at a 45° angle and fold over ¼". Fold in half lengthwise with wrong sides together and press.

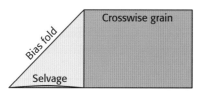

Bias Binding

1. Fold one corner of the fabric so that it forms a triangle. Cut along the folded line to create a bias edge.

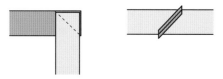

2. Using a see-through ruler, measure from the bias edge and cut strips 2½" wide. Continue cutting until you have enough strips to go around the perimeter of the quilt plus about 10".

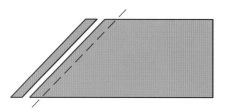

3. Join the strips end to end, using a ¼" seam allowance. Press the seams open.

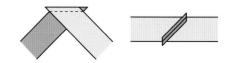

4. Fold the strip in half lengthwise, wrong sides together, and press. Fold one end over ¼" and press.

Attaching the Binding

1. Starting about 12" from one corner of the quilt, place the binding on the quilt top with right sides together and raw edges even.

2. Sew through all layers with a ¼"-wide seam allowance. Stop stitching ¼" from the corner and backstitch. Raise the presser foot and remove the quilt from the machine.

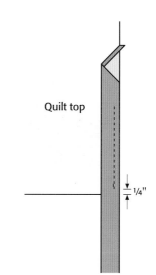

3. Fold the binding straight up, then straight down, even with the next edge to be sewn. Begin stitching ¼" from the corner. Continue stitching around each corner in the same manner.

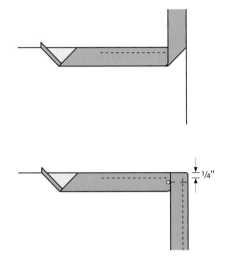

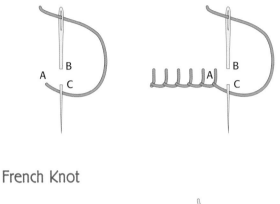

4. When you reach the starting point of the binding, trim it at an angle, leaving 1" to tuck into the beginning fold. Finish the seam.

5. Turn the binding over the raw edge of quilt and hand stitch to the quilt back.

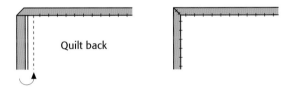

Quilt back

USING EMBROIDERY STITCHES

Use the following embroidery stitches to hand stitch the appliqué shapes to the background or to add embellishments to your project. The blanket stitch can also be done by machine if your sewing machine has this feature.

Blanket Stitch

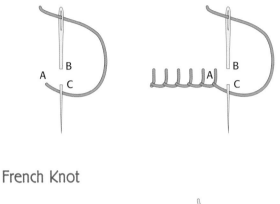

French Knot

Straight Stitch or Long Stitch

Stem Stitch

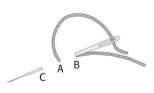

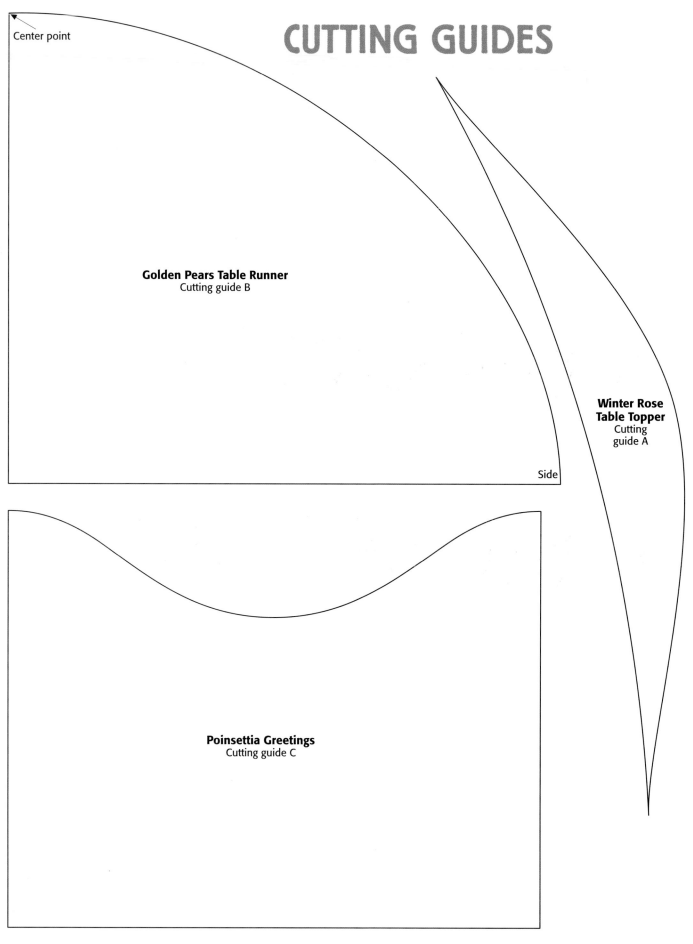

Center point

CUTTING GUIDES

Golden Pears Table Runner
Cutting guide B

Side

**Winter Rose
Table Topper**
Cutting
guide A

Poinsettia Greetings
Cutting guide C

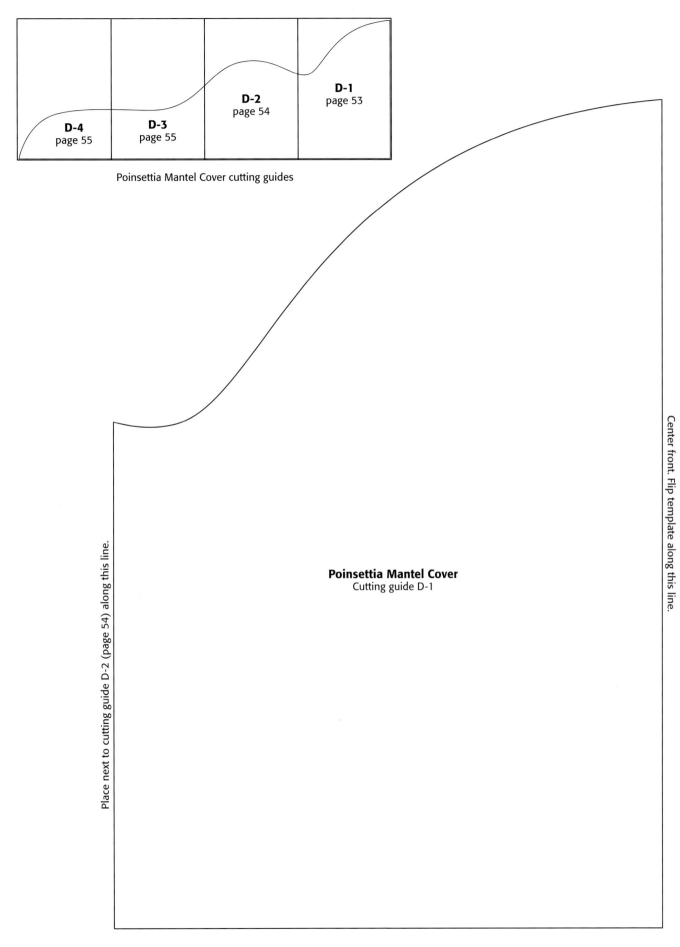

D-4
page 55

D-3
page 55

D-2
page 54

D-1
page 53

Poinsettia Mantel Cover cutting guides

Place next to cutting guide D-2 (page 54) along this line.

Center front. Flip template along this line.

Poinsettia Mantel Cover
Cutting guide D-1

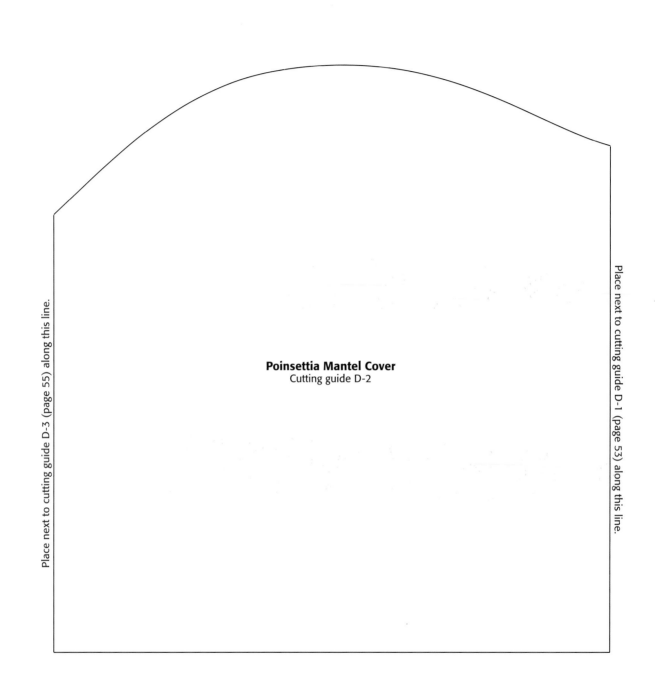

Poinsettia Mantel Cover
Cutting guide D-2

Place next to cutting guide D-3 (page 55) along this line.

Place next to cutting guide D-1 (page 53) along this line.

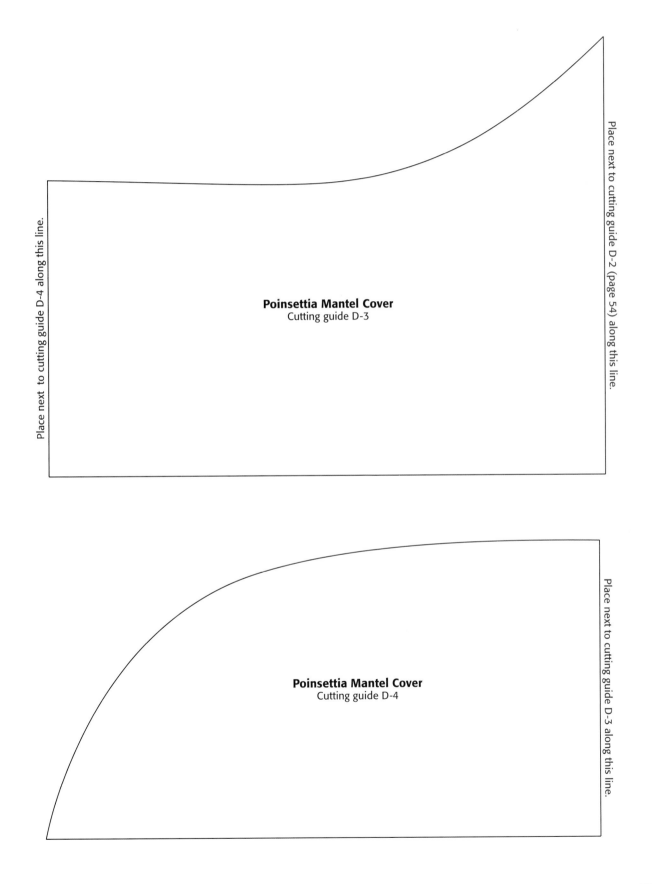

Place next to cutting guide D-4 along this line.

Place next to cutting guide D-2 (page 54) along this line.

Poinsettia Mantel Cover
Cutting guide D-3

Place next to cutting guide D-3 along this line.

Poinsettia Mantel Cover
Cutting guide D-4

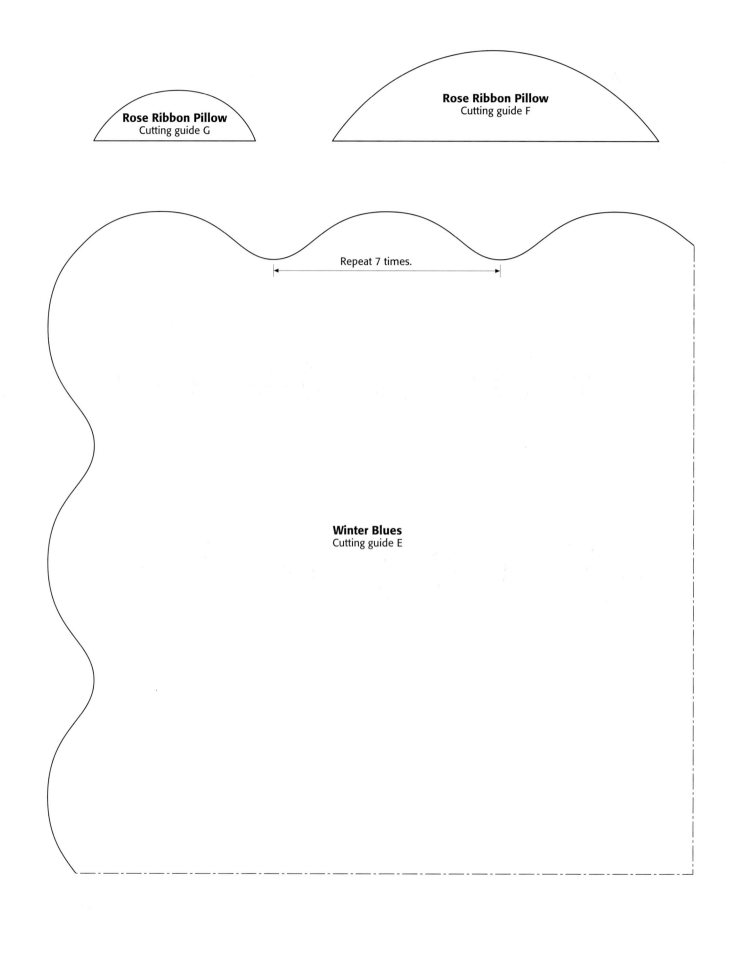

Rose Ribbon Pillow
Cutting guide G

Rose Ribbon Pillow
Cutting guide F

Repeat 7 times.

Winter Blues
Cutting guide E

TEMPLATES

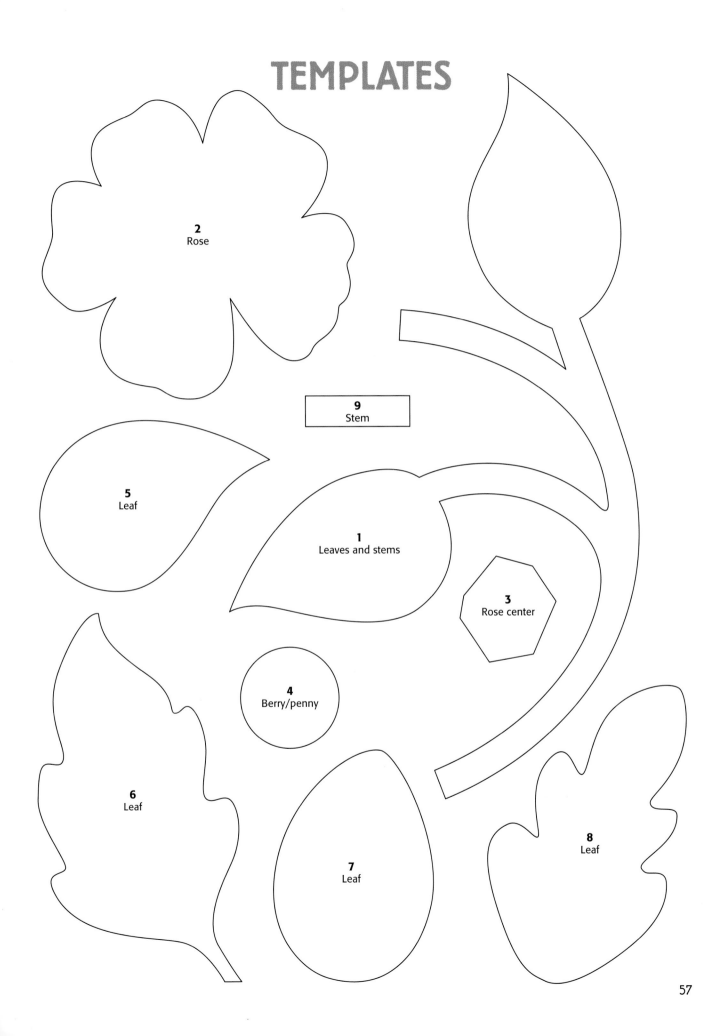

2
Rose

9
Stem

5
Leaf

1
Leaves and stems

3
Rose center

4
Berry/penny

6
Leaf

7
Leaf

8
Leaf

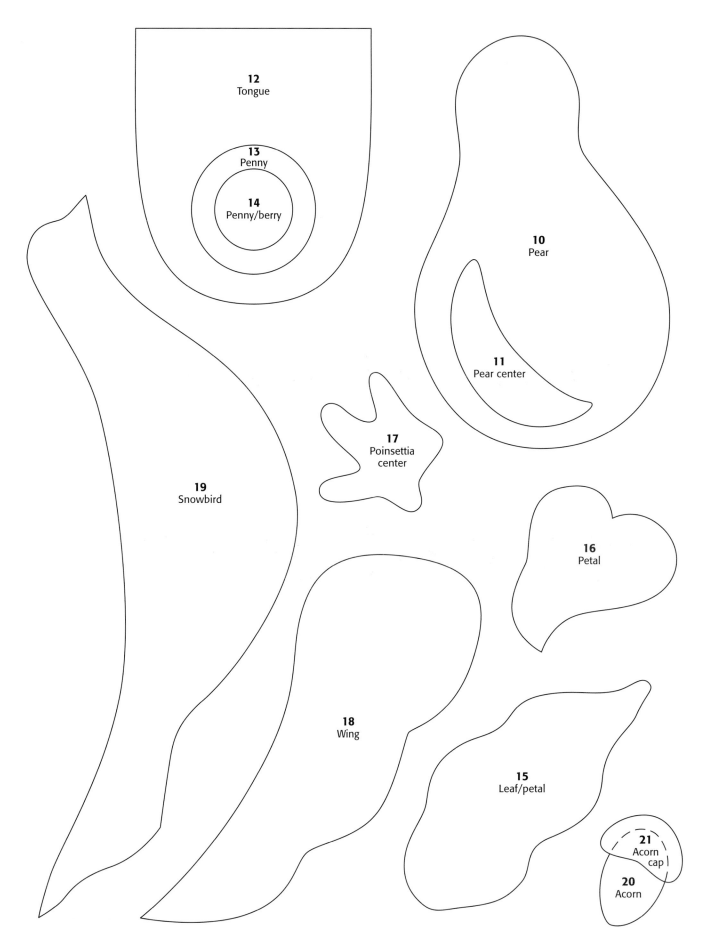

12
Tongue

13
Penny

14
Penny/berry

10
Pear

11
Pear center

17
Poinsettia
center

19
Snowbird

16
Petal

18
Wing

15
Leaf/petal

21
Acorn
cap

20
Acorn

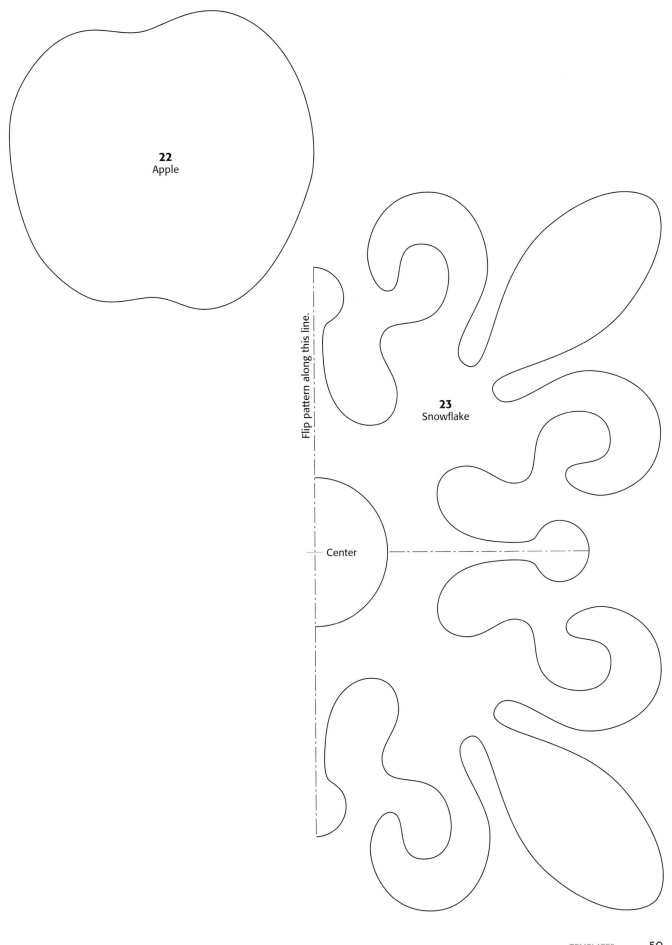

22
Apple

Flip pattern along this line.

23
Snowflake

Center

RESOURCES

A special thanks to the following companies that graciously donated materials to complete our book:

Hawthorne Gallery
245 East Main
Dayton, WA 99328
509-382-3137
Hawthorne Gallery is a retail source of wool felt,
    wool-felt kits, and quilting supplies.

National Nonwovens
PO Box 150
Easthampton, MA 01027
800-333-3469
National Nonwovens supplied the wonderful wool felt
    used in all of our projects—we love it!

Pfaff American Sales Corp.
610 Winters Avenue
Paramus, NJ 07652
201-262-7211
Pfaff supplied us with another fantastic sewing
    machine to help complete the book in record time!

YLI Corporation
161 W. Main Street
Rock Hill, SC 29730
803-985-3100
YLI supplied us with Jeanstitch topstitching thread,
    our favorite thread for blanket stitching.

REFERENCES

Following are a few of our favorite books that we think you, too, will find helpful and inspirational.

Brandt, Janet Carija. *Wool-on-Wool Folk Art Quilts.*
    Bothell, Wash.: That Patchwork Place, 1995.

Doak, Carol. *Your First Quilt Book (or it should be!).*
    Bothell, Wash.: That Patchwork Place, 1997.

Folk Art. Alexandria, Va.: Time-Life Books, 1990.

Hargrave, Harriet, *Heirloom Machine Quilting,*
    Lafayette, Calif: C&T Publishing, 1995.

Noble, Maurine. *Machine Quilting Made Easy.* Bothell,
    Wash.: That Patchwork Place, 1994.

Noble, Maurine, and Elizabeth Hendricks. *Machine
    Quilting with Decorative Threads.* Bothell, Wash.:
    That Patchwork Place, 1998.

Wells, Jean. *Buttonhole Stitch Appliqué.* Lafayette,
    Calif.: C & T Publishing, 1995.

ABOUT THE AUTHORS

Patti and Pam

Pamela Mostek and Patti Eaton met years ago when, as wives and mothers with young families, they discovered they shared the love of making just about anything, and the partnership began.

They joke that they have tried it all—from painting on furniture to painting on silk. They've done wedding coordinating, flower arranging, and even weaving. They've entered juried shows as watercolorists and county fairs as gardeners and crafters. Through it all, they have been the best of friends and creative partners.

About fifteen years ago, they discovered quilting.

Pam retired from her teaching career to work full-time in the quilting industry, and Patti expanded her retail business into a full-service quilt shop. Today, Pam spends her time designing for her pattern company, Making Lemonade Designs; writing books; and editing freelance in the quilting world. Patti keeps busy designing for her pattern company, Hawthorne Handworks, and running her quilt shop, Hawthorne Gallery.

One thing is for sure, they're both still smitten with the creative process. There will always be something new out there for them to try!

new and bestselling titles from

America's Best-Loved Craft & Hobby Books™

America's Best-Loved Quilt Books®

NEW RELEASES
Bear's Paw Plus
All Through the Woods
American Quilt Classics
Amish Wall Quilts
Animal Kingdom CD-ROM
Batik Beauties
The Casual Quilter
Fantasy Floral Quilts
Fast Fusible Quilts
Friendship Blocks
From the Heart
Log Cabin Fever
Machine-Stitched Cathedral Stars
Magical Hexagons
Quilts From Larkspur Farm
Potting Shed Patchwork
Repliqué Quilts
Successful Scrap Quilts
   From Simple Rectangles

APPLIQUÉ
Artful Album Quilts
Artful Appliqué
Colonial Appliqué
Red and Green: An Appliqué Tradition
Rose Sampler Supreme

BABY QUILTS
Easy Paper-Pieced Baby Quilts
Even More Quilts for Baby: Easy as ABC
More Quilts for Baby: Easy as ABC
Play Quilts
The Quilted Nursery
Quilts for Baby: Easy as ABC

HOLIDAY QUILTS
Christmas at That Patchwork Place
Holiday Collage Quilts
Paper Piece a Merry Christmas
A Snowman's Family Album Quilt
Welcome to the North Pole

LEARNING TO QUILT
Basic Quiltmaking Techniques for:
   Borders and Bindings
   Divided Circles
   Hand Appliqué
   Machine Appliqué
   Strip Piecing
The Joy of Quilting
The Simple Joys of Quilting
Your First Quilt Book (or it should be!)

PAPER PIECING
50 Fabulous Paper-Pieced Stars
For the Birds
Paper Piece a Flower Garden
Paper-Pieced Bed Quilts
Paper-Pieced Curves
A Quilter's Ark
Show Me How to Paper Piece

ROTARY CUTTING
101 Fabulous Rotary-Cut Quilts
365 Quilt Blocks a Year Perpetual Calendar
Around the Block Again
Biblical Blocks
Creating Quilts with Simple Shapes
Flannel Quilts
More Fat Quarter Quilts
More Quick Watercolor Quilts
Razzle Dazzle Quilts

SCRAP QUILTS
Nickel Quilts
Scrap Frenzy
Scrappy Duos
Spectacular Scraps

CRAFTS
The Art of Stenciling
Baby Dolls and Their Clothes
Creating with Paint
The Decorated Kitchen
The Decorated Porch
A Handcrafted Christmas
Painted Chairs
Sassy Cats

KNITTING & CROCHET
Too Cute!
Clever Knits
Crochet for Babies and Toddlers
Crocheted Sweaters
Fair Isle Sweaters Simplified
Irresistible Knits
Knit It Your Way
Knitted Shawls, Stoles, and Scarves
Knitted Sweaters for Every Season
Knitting with Novelty Yarns
Paintbox Knits
Simply Beautiful Sweaters
Simply Beautiful Sweaters for Men
The Ultimate Knitter's Guide

Our books are available at bookstores and your favorite craft, fabric and yarn retailers. If you don't see the title you're looking for, visit us at www.martingale-pub.com or contact us at:

1-800-426-3126
International: 1-425-483-3313

Fax: 1-425-486-7596

E-mail: info@martingale-pub.com

For more information and a full list of our titles, visit our
Web site or call for a free catalog.